Made in the USA
Monee, IL
12 June 2024

59735930R00057